The Carrot Nappers

By
Keith Large

Allotment Antics and
the Lure of the Love-shed

association

All proceeds to the Stroke Association

LASHEATH BOOKS

This book is dedicated
to the loving memory of my Mum,
to remember all the love
and laughs she gave

Acknowledgements

I wish to thank my writing friends Maria Smith, Daniel Ribot, Keith Morley, Brian Fury, Tony Gutteridge, Janet Newman, Janet Scrivens and Joyce Clarke, who travelled many miles on a dark November night to support the debut performance of 'The Carrot Nappers'. Along with much appreciation to the many people who supported our sell-out Conquer Stroke New Writing Night at The Y Theatre in Leicester in March 2016, in support of The Stroke Association. With particular thanks to our celebrity guests, award-winning actor Jeff Stewart, and ITV Central Weather presenter Lucy Kite, with her wonderful warmth and professionalism in compering the evening.

First published by LASHEATH Books in Great Britain 2016
Printed by York Publishing Services Ltd.
Design and production by keith@antcreative.com www.antcreative.com.
Cover illustration: Matthew Shaw

The Carrot Nappers

by

Keith Large

Contents

The Carrot Nappers was first performed as a rehearsed reading in front of a full house at The ADC Theatre in Cambridge in November 2009, before going on to headline The Belper Short Play Festival in June 2012 as a full production. Since then, due to caring for my mum when she became ill in July 2012, until she tragically passed away after suffering a stroke in August 2015, this play script has been lying in the Love-shed awaiting its next stage run. Now we have the opportunity to publish it in print and share the laughs with fans who enjoyed it both as a stage play and in its earlier form as a published magazine short story. At the same time proceeds from this publication will raise funds for the Stroke Association and their marvellous work helping both stroke survivors and stroke prevention.

Enter the Love-shed and enjoy…

Synopsis

Vinnie Hollis is an out-of-work nightclub bouncer, desperate for any work in the recession-hit town of Coalshed. Employed by pensioner Albert Jackson to guard Topside Allotments 17 foot prize carrot on the eve of a big competition, Vinnie foils an attempt by Topside's rivals Onion-Head and Weed-killer Willie to nap the carrot, only to discover they steal it at the show when Vinnie's not there. Albert once again enlists the help of Vinnie and his flirtatious lover Lisa to set up a honey-trap in Topside's famous

'Love-shed', to snare Onion-Head and recover the prize carrot.

Character List

VINNIE HOLLIS is a feared man in Coalshed. An ex-nightclub bouncer. Aged 40, Vinnie is looking for work to fund his favourite pastime – womanising.

ALBERT JACKSON is retired and the secretary of Topside Allotments. Aged 66, Albert is a tad too old to recover the theft of Topside's prize 17-foot carrot.

ONION-HEAD, like Vinnie, is a real lady's man. Though after leaving Topside under a cloud, Albert is convinced Onion-Head is channelling his energy into sabotaging Topside's chances in prize gardening competitions. Vinnie believes the 50-year-old still has an eye for the ladies and can be enticed to return to the Love-shed.

LISA is the love of Vinnie's life, despite her living with another man. Aged 30, she enjoys being spoilt by Vinnie and the excitement of their dangerous trysts. Flirtatious and beautiful, she is the perfect accomplice in trapping Onion-Head.

The Carrot Nappers

The play takes place at Topside Allotments, Coalshed. Autumn.

(Song of Amazonia Music – 55 seconds)

2.30 p.m. Monday afternoon

An angry Vinnie Hollis, clutching a copy of 'The Coalshed Echo', is digesting the headline:
CARROT NAPPERS GET TOPSIDE OF BOUNCER.
Vinnie looks to see if there is anybody on the allotment before making a call on his mobile phone.

Vinnie: Albert, what the bloody hell is going on?

Albert Jackson is hiding behind the runner beans, praying Vinnie doesn't see or hear him.

Albert: (whispers) We've been had, Vinnie.
Vinnie: Speak up, you old git.
Albert: (slightly louder) We've been had, Vinnie.
Vinnie: We've? How about I've? Do you know how damaging it is for an out-of-work nightclub bouncer to have his name plastered across a newspaper saying he now can't guard a carrot?
Albert: Vinnie, believe me, I know how you feel. We've had to hand the trophy back because the carrot we won with wasn't real.
Vinnie: So they swapped the carrots at the show?
Albert: It must have been when everyone went off to watch Alan Titchmarsh.
Vinnie: But the paper's saying it got napped when I was on guard overnight at Topside.
Albert: You know what The Coalshed Echo is like. They once printed Coalshed United were top of Division Eight.

9

	Then they had to admit they'd published the league table upside down.
Vinnie:	Mud sticks.
Albert:	Pity it didn't to our prize carrot – we'd have identified it better.
Vinnie:	Identify it? The bloody thing was 17 feet long and it got stolen before your eyes.
Albert:	I'll get onto The Coalshed Echo now and demand they publish a full correction that it wasn't pinched under your guard.
Vinnie:	After you've picked me some runner beans.

Vinnie starts to walk towards the runner beans.

Albert:	Tell me you can't see me hiding.
Vinnie:	No, but I can hear you now you're speaking up.

Vinnie pulls back the runner bean leaves to reveal Albert.

Albert:	Don't hurt me 'cos I've not paid you yet.
Vinnie:	Do you think I'd hit an old man?
Albert:	No, but I'd like you to hit whoever napped our carrot.
Vinnie:	Who do you think it is? Weed-killer Willie and that Onion-Head again?
Albert:	Without a doubt. I seen them flogging their Alan Titchmarsh tickets.

Vinnie looks over to the shed.

Vinnie:	When I caught them down at Topside I should have locked them in this shed all weekend, instead of marching them down to the Church's Harvest Festival with your leftovers.

Vinnie's phone starts ringing

Vinnie: Oh, hello sweetheart. No I didn't fall asleep on
             the job.

Vinnie throws his phone at the shed, turning back to Albert
in a rage.

Vinnie: See? Even one of my girlfriends thinks I can't last
             the night now.
Albert: Which one was it?
Vinnie: Lisa, and she's my favourite. I've spent a fortune on
             her. Can only get her out on a Tuesday night when
             her boyfriend goes to his Airfix model club.
Albert: Isn't she available in the day?
Vinnie: She is, but she likes her candlelit dinners. All the
             pubs and restaurants around here do in the day is
             Faggots and Peas on two for the price of one. Not
             exactly the wining and dining technique you saw
             Nigel Havers use in The Charmer.

Albert looks over to the shed. (Two chairs)

Albert: You could always invite her over for salmon and
             champagne in the shed.
Vinnie: Are you real? It'd be bloody freezing in the winter.
Albert: Far more chance she'd want you to keep her warm in
             there.
Vinnie: You speak like a man of experience.
Albert: They don't call that the 'Love-shed' for nothing.
             Tomatoes aren't the only fruity things we've had in
             there. Something magical about ladies and that shed.
             Onion-Head's never had the same success as a lady's
             man since he left Topside.
Vinnie: Onion-Head used to have an allotment here?
Albert: Until we had to ban him 'cos we couldn't get him
             out of the 'Love-shed'. His plot became so overgrown
             with weeds, and we could never get in there to put
             our spades away.

Vinnie:	Get rid of him easy enough?
Albert:	No; it's not like your profession where you just sling 'em out – had to go through the committee disciplinary process. Nobody had the balls to try and get rid of him on the grounds he was spending too long in the 'Love-shed' hardening his cucumber. We went at him on the overgrown weeds angle. That's when I think he got in touch with this 'Weed-killer Willie' guy.
Vinnie:	He sorted his plot out?
Albert:	Think so.
Vinnie:	So how did you get rid of him then?
Albert:	Padlocked him in the 'Love-shed' just as his wife was coming to tell him his tea was ready.
Vinnie:	Bet that went down well.
Albert:	She stopped him renting a plot here.
Vinnie:	Didn't stop him though. I used to be on the door at some singles nights and he'd turn up wearing his wedding ring.
Albert:	He's on a different agenda these days in the gardening world. It's beat Topside at all costs. He's one of our most wanted carrot nappers.
Vinnie:	Leopards don't change their spots, Albert; once a lady's man, always a lady's man.
Albert:	I don't like to disagree with a bloke your size Vinnie, but I'm going to have to. When a Romeo turns into a carrot napper, even Demi Moore emerging from the sea in her itsy-bitsy two-piece couldn't distract him from napping a prize red-top.
Vinnie:	Lisa would, if you lured him back down to the 'Love-shed'.
Albert:	I don't think you'd get her down here after the way you put the phone down on her.
Vinnie:	She'll be fine. We'll make it up. She knows it's the stress of me being unemployed.
Albert:	You think she'd be willing to set up a honey trap for Onion-Head?

Vinnie: If you supplied the salmon and champagne.
Albert: I was only joking about that. It'd be more likely all
            Topside could offer her is elderflower cordial and
            marrow soup.
Vinnie: Well, you better forget that idea then... and getting
            your prize carrot back.
Albert: Ok, maybe we could up it to strawberry wine and
            cherry tomatoes.
Vinnie: I can see you know how to treat a lady, Albert. I bet
            when Fred Astaire walked in the dance hall and saw
            you there he thought, "I'll never pull a Ginger if I've
            got to compete with Albert 'Charmer' Jackson."
Albert: Ok, maybe we could stretch to salmon and cider.
Vinnie: Cider? What make?
Albert: It'll be homemade with apples from that tree over
            there.

Vinnie and Albert look over to the tree.

Vinnie: An apple tree?
Albert: Apples make cider.
Vinnie: Not when they look like conkers they don't.
Albert: I don't believe it – someone's napped the apple tree.
Vinnie: And replaced it with a conker tree?
Albert: Yes.
Vinnie: They'd have needed a crane.
Albert: Plenty available now the building trade's slack.

Vinnie turns to look at the Love-shed.

Vinnie: Now are you sure that's the original Love-shed?
            Otherwise Onion-Head might say he's got a
            headache.
Albert: Oh don't worry – the base of the Love-shed's
            fastened down with anchor bolts.
Vinnie: I hope there's none been put in upside down, or the
            69 position might become the 999 position.

Albert: I did get a sore bum once in there, but I thought it was another version of unprotected sex.

Vinnie: You mean you've christened the Love-shed as well? You dirty old man.

Albert: I was a lot younger when I tried it out.

Vinnie: I bet you was married when you did it.

Albert: I'm not proud of it – like Onion-Head and you are.

Vinnie: C'mon, what was her name? Brenda Brussell or Randy Rhubarb?

Albert: I'm not telling you her name, because the wife's sister's not got a common one.

Vinnie: Bloody hell, I thought I'd seen it all working on the doors, but there's no woman safe when you watering-can brigade start getting your fertilizers out.

Albert: Look – I was having a difficult period in my life.

Vinnie: You mean the wife's idea of an early night became a cup of Horlicks?

Albert: No – my tomatoes stayed green and my carrots kept running off with the rabbits.

Vinnie: So once Bugs Bunny stopped pinching your red-tops you became pure again?

Albert: Yes, and I've remained so ever since.

Vinnie: But now you're getting your carrots napped again so, if history repeats itself, it's mums lock up your grandmas – Albert Jackson's loved up on strawberry wine.

Albert: You can laugh. I think it's about time you went in to bat and serenaded the lovely Lisa down here.

Vinnie: Don't forget we've got to entice Onion-Head as well.

Albert: We'll start with a PO Box number in 'The Big Carrot'.

Vinnie: What's that when it's at home?

Albert: It's Coalshed's underground gardening magazine. Excuse the pun, but it's got a seedy side.

Vinnie: Explain!

Albert: Some read it because they're gardeners and some read it for the bits you find between the lettuce and

	the broccoli.
Vinnie:	You mean they're looking for seconds.
Albert:	Used to be thirds and fourths before Onion-Head got obsessed with napping our carrots.
Vinnie:	I think it's about time we asked Lisa if she's up to the challenge.

Vinnie gets hold of his mobile phone again. Lisa's mobile rings.

Vinnie:	How do you fancy leading a real baddie on?
Lisa:	I don't. I get bored waiting for them coming out on parole.
Vinnie:	They're not all inside, you know.
Lisa:	They will be when slamming a phone down becomes a crime.
Vinnie:	Babe, I'm sorry about that. I'm under pressure. I need your help.
Lisa:	Need? It's always about what you need. You need to grow up and find yourself a wife and a proper job.
Vinnie:	(whispers) Close your ears, Albert.

Vinnie walks away from Albert.

Vinnie:	Wife? You know I can't find myself another wife. It's too risky. My second wife nearly found out I'm still married to the first one.
Lisa:	Well, I've no intention of becoming your third wife whilst you're still married to both of them.
Vinnie:	I don't want you to be my wife. I want you to make out you might like to become somebody else's wife.
Lisa:	Where's your charm gone? It seems to have disappeared with that carrot. First you slam the phone down on me and now I'm not good enough to be your wife.
Vinnie:	Oh c'mon, you're over-reacting. You're far too good for me. As you say, I've not even got a proper job.

Lisa:	Be serious, Vinnie. You can't call guarding a carrot a proper job.
Vinnie:	It's not easy work, you know.
Lisa:	Not when it's 17 foot and you still can't keep hold of it.
Vinnie:	Well I'm trying to give you the chance to do better.
Lisa:	What do you mean, do better?
Vinnie:	You catch the carrot napper and get the carrot back.
Lisa:	Oh, this is where leading this bloke on comes in. You want me to get him thinking I'd like to become Mrs Lisa Carrot.
Vinnie:	More like Mrs Lisa Onion-Head.
Lisa:	I'm not being called that.
Vinnie:	You won't be. Because you've not got to marry him, you've just got to get him in the Love-shed.
Lisa:	With his carrot?
Vinnie:	No, it'll be too big to get in there.
Lisa:	Is it really? You know Vinnie, I've always had a motto when it comes to men.
Vinnie:	What's that?
Lisa:	Never judge them by their name.
Vinnie:	So you'll do it? You'll chat Onion-Head up?
Lisa:	I will. He sounds fun.
Vinnie:	He's not fun. He's a carrot napper.
Lisa:	Calm down Vinnie; jealousy won't get your 17-footer back.

Vinnie ends the call and runs back to Albert.

Vinnie:	Albert, she said she'd do it. Get that advert in 'The Big Carrot'.
Albert:	It's very near the deadline for this week's edition, but I'm sure if I promise them a few runner beans on top of the going rate, they'll get it in.
Vinnie:	What are you waiting for? Phone it through now.
Albert:	I can't.
Vinnie:	What do you mean, you can't?

Albert:	We've not got a PO Box number.
Vinnie:	Address it care of the Love-shed.
Albert:	Onion-Head will never send anything here.
Vinnie:	Can we put a photo in with the advert?
Albert:	I think I could swing it if we offered them a bag of my best King Eddie's and a couple of elephant-trunk-size marrows.
Vinnie:	Trust me. When he sees how beautiful Lisa is, he'll be writing in.
Albert:	How are you going to get a photo in this quick?
Vinnie:	Who's Onion-Head's dream woman?
Albert:	Anyone that will go out with him.
Vinnie:	C'mon – he must have a favourite.
Albert:	He's always had this thing about Raquel Welch. Reckoned he kept going out with different women until he found one that lived up to her.
Vinnie:	And did he ever find one?
Albert:	No – wife stopped play.
Vinnie:	She's not. I've told you the covers have come off and he's been up them singles nights.
Albert:	So does Lisa look like Raquel Welch?
Vinnie:	She will on the photo 'The Big Carrot' will be taking off the One Million Years BC website.
Albert:	I'm not sure they're allowed to do that.

Vinnie looks over to the row of parsnips.

| Vinnie: | Look – offer them some of them prize parsnips over there and they'll publish it in whatever size you like. |

Vinnie passes Albert his mobile phone.

| Vinnie: | Here – go in the Love-shed and make the call. |

Albert disappears into the Love-shed. Vinnie starts assessing the runner beans and the conker tree for places to hide.

Vinnie: (*talking to himself*) I think I'll hide behind the conker tree and throw a few at him, just before Lisa naps his onions.

Albert reappears from the Love-shed.

Albert: It's done. I had to throw in a few raspberries as well, but it'll be in tomorrow's 'Big Carrot'.

Vinnie looks over to the Love-shed door.

Vinnie: Good job this door's got a letterbox.

Albert: Don't worry; the postman knows where to come. I have all my magazines delivered here that I don't want my wife to see.

Vinnie: You're as bad as Onion-Head.

Albert: I'm not. At least I buy them. He pinches his from the library.

Vinnie: You can't get them type in the library.

Albert: You can, but you're not allowed to borrow them.

Vinnie: Bet that's cos' the librarians want a crafty read.

Albert: Oh, they do. They love reading about steam railways. My wife thinks the magazines are a waste of money, but you've got to have something to read if your lover gets delayed getting to the Love-shed.

Vinnie: I hope Lisa's not going to find you in here on the wrong track when she brings Onion-Head back.

Albert: I'm only joking. I've told you I've not derailed for years. I retired after a jealous husband tried to comb my hair with a rake.

Vinnie: I think we better retire from here for the day. Can you leave me a spare key to the Love-shed so I can check the post?

Albert: Check the post? I know your game. You want to lock yourself in with this month's Steam Railway.

Vinnie clenches his fist.

Vinnie: Do you want this carrot back?

Albert hands him a key and begins to leave the allotment.

Vinnie: Make sure you put a copy of 'The Big Carrot'
through the Love-shed letterbox as soon as
it's on sale.
Albert: I will.

Albert leaves the allotment. Vinnie begins to make a call on
his mobile phone to Lisa. Lisa's mobile rings.

Vinnie: How do you fancy spending tonight in the
Love-shed?
Lisa: Is this Onion-Head and his big carrot there already?
Vinnie: No; there'll be just you and me. I thought I could
help you get familiar with the Love-shed.
Lisa: Oh Vinnie, I can't get out. I can't keep telling my
boyfriend I'm going for driving lessons every night
– especially when he finds out I passed my test six
months ago.
Vinnie: You mean they're repeating Pride and Prejudice on
the TV?
Lisa: Don't get like that. I'm doing this Onion-Head job
for you.
Vinnie: I'm sorry. I know I'm being miserable. Times are
hard with no work on the doors.
Lisa: Why don't you sleep overnight in the Love-shed?
Save on your gas and electric. Bet they've got some
fruit you can pinch from the allotment.
Vinnie: Plenty of conkers.
Lisa: They'll make sure you stay a hard man.
Vinnie: On that note, I think I'll follow your advice and stay
here until the postman brings some 'desperately
seeking sunflower' applications from these
cauliflower Romeos.

Vinnie ends the call and goes inside the Love-shed to sleep.
He's still asleep as daylight breaks. Entering the
edge of the allotments is Onion-Head, muttering
to himself.

Onion-Head: That's one advantage of slipping the editor a few
onions; you get a copy of 'The Big Carrot' before
anybody else. Risky me coming here, but when
there's a Raquel Welch lookalike involved I need to
be the first to get my Love CV in. This is much faster
than putting a stamp on it.

Onion-Head starts walking towards the Love-shed.

Onion-Head: I'd better be quiet now. There might be some tramp
sleeping in here.

Onion-Head puts an envelope through the letterbox. Vinnie is still
fast asleep. Onion-Head tiptoes back out of the allotments. Vinnie
finally wakes up. Vinnie discovers the envelope and gets on the
phone to Albert. Albert's mobile rings.

Vinnie:	He must have been sitting outside the newsagents.
Albert:	He's never got his letter in already. What's he using? Super-special delivery?
Vinnie:	No, it looks like it's come by hand. I've only just got here. I must have just missed him.
Albert:	Pity you didn't stay the night in the Love-shed. You'd have heard him. Then you could have kidnapped him until we got the carrot back.
Vinnie:	That would have saved us involving Lisa.
Albert:	Proves he's still chasing the ladies. And he's not frightened to approach the Love-shed.
Vinnie:	I've told you, Albert; once a lady's man, always a lady's man.
Albert:	What's he put in his letter?

Vinnie picks up the letter and reads from it.

Vinnie: Is this man real? Dear Raquel, in the gardening
            world I'm known as Onion-Head after making a few
            million selling quality cloves of garlic to the French
            to improve their onion soup. I'm of Italian blood
            and I was born Valentino Polo. I've an athletic body,
            I'm romantic, rich, caring, handsome, and I've got
            the biggest carrot – as you'll know from borrowing
            the Love-shed for an address. Hope you are genuine
            because I am. If so and you want to be loved like
            you've never been loved before, e-mail your phone
            number to Onionhead@bigcarrot.com

Albert: If he's Italian, that conker tree will grow apples
            again. Is Lisa ok about giving her mobile phone
            number out to him?

Vinnie: Yes, she'll put an Ivor Biggun ringtone to his number
            so she'll know it's him calling.

Albert: I've a mate at the computer shop who can set up a
            one-off e-mail address to send Onion-Head her phone
            number. We'll send it from Lisa@theLove-shed.com

Vinnie: I'll leave you to get on with it.

Albert: Before you go, what's the actual plan when Lisa gets
            Onion-Head back to the Love-shed?

Vinnie: Once she's got his clothes off and throws them out
            to us, he'll have a few hours to get the prize carrot
            back to Topside – or else we'll be sending his dirty
            washing to Mrs Onion-Head.

Albert: It'll be interesting if he has to go out naked to fetch
            the carrot.

Vinnie: If he's got any sense he'll get Weed-killer Willie to
            bring it down.

Albert: I'm not sure he'll come down to Topside if he knows
            you're around.

Vinnie: Who's going to tell him I'm about? We'll let Lisa do
            the negotiating.

Albert: Smart move. I'll go and get that e-mail sent.

Vinnie presses the end call button only for his phone to ring again.

Lisa:	I'm bored.
Vinnie:	Shouldn't you be at work?
Lisa:	I knew from the minute I stood at the wrong bus stop I wasn't going to make it into the office today.
Vinnie:	You want to look after your job – there's not many about.
Lisa:	My boss wouldn't sack me. Who do you think tells his wife he's had to go abroad on business when he spends the whole weekend at the 19th hole at Coalshed golf club?
Vinnie:	Well you're about to get a call from another slimy character – though he might call himself Valentino Polo.
Lisa:	I think it's about time I saw this Love-shed then.
Vinnie:	You better get down here before he phones up. And make sure you're standing at the right bus stop.
Lisa:	It's ok, I'll get a taxi. This Onion-Head will be paying for it. Or else when I get hold of his onions his eyes will water like a sprinkler on overtime.

Lisa arrives at Topside Allotments with her mobile phone.

Vinnie:	That was quick.
Lisa:	Smile nicely at the right cab driver and they put their foot down for you.
Vinnie:	I bet they do. Anyway, has he rung yet?
Lisa:	How's he got my phone number?
Vinnie:	Albert's e-mailing it to him.
Lisa:	The bloke's not liable to be sat at his computer all day checking his e-mails unless he's a real sad Ken.

Lisa'S phone begins to ring.

Vinnie:	That's him. See? He is a sad Ken.
Lisa:	Hello, who's that?

Albert: It's Albert. Is that Lisa?

Lisa: I can be whoever you want me to be.

Albert: It is Lisa.

Lisa: Seeing as you're going to be paying my wages
            I better be.

Vinnie: Is that Albert? Tell him to get off the phone.
            He's blocking the phone line up. Onion-Head could
            be trying to get through.

Lisa covers the mouthpiece of her phone and turns to speak
to Vinnie.

Lisa: I don't think there's a phone line on the end
            of a mobile.

Vinnie: You know what I mean. C'mon, you're wasting time.

Lisa moves her phone back to speak to Albert.

Lisa: Anyway Albert, what can I do for you?

Albert: Oh I'm just checking I e-mailed Onion-Head the
            right number.

Lisa: And you e-mailed him the right woman. I'll get
            your carrot back. Bye.

Lisa presses the end call button on her phone and turns to Vinnie.

Lisa: You better disappear in case he's hiding around the
            corner when he makes his call.

Vinnie: I'll hide behind the conker tree.

Lisa: When I get him here, stay hidden until I've had time
            to seduce the carrot out of him.

Vinnie: As long as you don't put yourself in any danger.
            What words are you going to shout when you need
            me to step in?

Lisa: 'Orgasmic Onions.'

Vinnie goes to hide behind the conker tree. Lisa'S mobile phone begins to ring.

Lisa:	Hello.
Onion-Head:	Are you the lady looking for a big carrot?
Lisa:	You could say that.
Onion-Head:	I bet you're not alone in that Love-shed.
Lisa:	Oh, I am. Nobody's been seen gardening at Topside since they lost the big competition. You know what bad losers some men can be.
Onion-Head:	Are you a member of Topside?
Lisa:	Oh no, I just borrow the Love-shed when I fancy a bit of fun.
Onion-Head:	I had years of making my marrow grow in there.
Lisa:	You sound like a man of experience. The type I like. Leave the virgins and the mummy's boys for the agony aunts to sort out. I like a lover who's loved a lot.
Onion-Head:	That's me. I've one thousand and fifty-two notches on my showcase turnip.
Lisa:	Now I don't want you getting completely the wrong idea. I don't want to be just another notch on your turnip. I want you to charm me with your success, both in and out of the Love-shed.
Onion-Head:	Are you sure there's nobody down at Topside?
Lisa:	Positive.
Onion-Head:	I'll bring you a photo of my 17ft carrot. The one Topside copied with a plastic one and got disqualified.
Lisa:	So won't I ever get to see your real carrot?
Onion-Head:	Well, that depends on what happens in the Love-shed.
Lisa:	I'd better make sure you have a good time in here then. I can't wait to see this photo.
Onion-Head:	I'm on my way now.
Lisa:	Use Formula One Taxis – you'll be here in no time.

Onion-Head: I always use them. They let me stick my carrot out of
the back of their eight-seater.

Lisa: See you in a few minutes.

Lisa ends the call on her mobile phone and shouts over to Vinnie.

Lisa: Sounds like my friends at Formula One Taxis might
have a good idea where the prize carrot has been
delivered to. If we need them to talk, a few nails near
their tyres and they'll soon be talking carrots.

Vinnie: That's good to know. Better keep quiet. He'll be here
any second. Their taxis never stop at red lights.

Vinnie goes back behind the conker tree. Onion-Head arrives
wearing a T-shirt displaying the words
'the bigger the carrot, the better the lover'.
Lisa is waiting inside the Love-shed.
Onion-Head knocks on the door.

Onion-Head: It's your lucky day, baby. All your Richard Geres,
Colin Firths and Johnny Depps have arrived in
one man.

Lisa opens the Love-shed door and looks past Onion-Head.

Onion-Head: Who you looking for? There's not somebody else
about, is there?

Lisa: There's supposed to be a man about who can look
like Richard Gere, Colin Firth and Johnny Depp all
at the same time.

Onion-Head: That's me.

Lisa: No, you're having me on. You're much better looking
than those three.

Onion-Head: That's why I'm Onion-Head – King in a bed.

Lisa: What a pity there's no bed in the Love-shed
at the moment.

Onion-Head: The tight sods. Have they never replaced it after it
           got broke when Patricia Parsnip and me were going
           at it six times a night?

Lisa: Six times? I hope you're going to be gentler with me.
           I like to get to know a man first. I like to know how
           his mind works – what makes him successful. I find
           it such a great aphrodisiac.

Onion-Head: Success – it's second nature to me.

Lisa: I think you'd better step inside the Love-shed and
           tell me all about it. Do you mind if we leave the door
           open? It's very hot today.

Onion-Head: It is. In fact I think I'll take my shirt off.

Onion-Head takes his shirt off and Lisa takes hold of it as they
both step inside the Love-shed.

Lisa: Let me read the words on your chest. 'The bigger the
           carrot, the better the lover'. I'm fascinated by your
           success with carrots.

Onion-Head: Most women are. Ladies love a man who eats plenty
           of carrots.

Lisa: We do.

Onion-Head: Ever since it became known carrots make you see in
           the dark.

Lisa: Means you can do it without the lights on.

Onion-Head: And when we say you're beautiful you know we're
           telling the truth.

Vinnie makes a being sick noise from behind the conker tree.

Onion-Head: Did you hear that? It sounded like someone was
           being sick. Are you sure we're not alone?

Lisa: Relax. If there was anybody around your carrot eyes
           would have spotted them.

Onion-Head: This is dangerous territory for me you know.

Lisa: I can get very excited by danger.

Vinnie throws a conker at the Love-shed roof.

Onion-Head: I'm telling you there's somebody about.
Lisa: It's not your wife, is it?
Onion-Head: If she ever catches me in here again…
Lisa: There's every possibility if…
Onion-Head: If what?
Lisa: If the Love-shed's CCTV is switched on.
Onion-Head: They've not got cameras in here?
Lisa: Oh, they've got them all over the allotments –
since they've had a few carrots napped.
Onion-Head: This is one of them what-d'ya-call-its – a honey trap.
Lisa: Oh, it will be when I let the bees out.
Onion-Head: You think I'm a bloody carrot napper.
Lisa: Of course I don't. You're a lover not a napper…
I think.
Onion-Head: I am. Believe me, I'm not a napper.
Lisa: I think you need to prove it.
Onion-Head: Prove what?
Lisa: Prove you're a lover, Valentino Polo.
Onion-Head: I will but not here. I don't feel comfortable here.
Lisa: No man's ever turned me down in the Love-shed…
and left with his onions unpeeled.
Onion-Head: I'm not turning you down. You just deserve so much
better than a shed without a bed.

Vinnie makes another sick noise from behind the conker tree.

Onion-Head: There's that noise again.
Lisa: Stop changing the subject.
Onion-Head: Look, I can take you to a four and half star hotel –
the Coalshed Moathouse. It's got everything, ten
point eight kilowatt shower, enough complimentary
biscuits to fill your handbag with, and it would still
have a four-poster bed if I'd paid the repair bill.

Lisa: I don't want your fancy hotels. I want the Love-shed.
I thought you liked me because I looked like Raquel
Welch in One Million Years BC.

Onion-Head: I do.

Lisa: Prove it then. Show us your onions.

Onion-Head: I'm not peeling any more layers off in here.

Lisa: I think you've got something to hide inside them
trousers.

Onion-Head: I've not; I never hide my money in my underpants.

Lisa: I think you're hiding a miniature model of the prize
carrot.

Onion-Head: I've told you I'm not a carrot napper.

Lisa: Well, you're not a lover. You're a fake. In fact, I'm
going to report you to every lover's authority going.
The swinger's complaints committee will hear about
this. And the speed-dating Ombudsman. And I'll get
you banned from the last dance at every Coalshed
disco.

Onion-Head: With threats like that I've got no choice. Promise you
won't let them bees out.

Vinnie: Get on with it. Because if another conker hits me on
the head I'll come and pull 'em down myself.

Onion-Head: I'm telling you. There's somebody here.

Lisa: There's not. Now are they coming down or shall I
start reporting you?

Onion-Head: I'll need a massive cabbage leaf to protect my
modesty.

Vinnie makes his way from the conker tree and picks up a small
lettuce leaf along the way and heads for the Love-shed.

Vinnie: Sod this, I'm not waiting any longer.

Lisa sees Vinnie coming and turns to Onion-Head.

Lisa: Too late; looks like there is somebody here.

Onion-Head: Oh my slug-infested mushrooms! It's Vinnie Hollis. Vinnie; it's not what you think.

Vinnie: I know that – I've seen more action from two celibates doing a crossword.

Vinnie hands Onion-Head the small lettuce leaf.

Vinnie: Here, get them trousers off and cover yourself up with this.

Onion-Head: What do you want my trousers off for?

Vinnie: To send them to your wife if you don't get Formula One Taxis down here with Topside's 17ft carrot.

Onion-Head: I'm warning you – if you hit me, it's all on CCTV.

Vinnie: I'm warning you, if you don't take them trousers off it won't be some sweet honey bees inspecting your onions – it'll be a ferret looking for a dance partner.

Onion-Head: Please – not the one they keep at the Coalshed rescue centre?

Vinnie: No – the one I keep behind the conker tree.

Onion-Head: I'm only going to take them off if you close the door. And Lisa stands outside.

Lisa: I'm not standing outside now I know there's a ferret about.

Onion-Head: Well promise you'll close your eyes.

Lisa: OK, I Promise I'll close my eyes. No wonder they kicked you out of the Love-shed.

Vinnie: C'mon get on with it, before them "pretend to water the tomatoes" brigade get down here to escape their wives and listen to the Test Match.

The Love-shed door closes with Onion-Head and Lisa inside. The door slightly opens and Onion-Head'S hand passes his trousers to Vinnie.

Vinnie: Lisa, are you coming out?

Lisa: No – Onion-Head needs me to hold his leaf.

Vinnie: That could be tricky if you've got to keep your
               eyes shut.
Onion-Head: So when do I get my trousers back?
Lisa: Hopefully not yet.
Vinnie: When you get that 17ft prize carrot back.
Onion-Head: What makes you think I know where it is?
Vinnie: This ferret that's outside the door.
Onion-Head: What happens if my mate Weed-killer Willie has
               eaten the carrot?
Vinnie: Then we'll lock you in the Love-shed until your wife
               reports you missing and offers a reward.
Onion-Head: But she'll offer a reward to keep me missing.
Vinnie: She will in a few minutes when I take her these
               trousers.

Vinnie locks the Love-shed.

Onion-Head: No! Please don't lock me in! I'm sure he wasn't
               planning on mass producing his carrot cakes until
               next week. Please, somebody just lend me a mobile
               phone.

Vinnie passes his mobile phone into the Love-shed. Onion-Head
phones Weed-Killer Willie.

Onion-Head: (in a high-pitched voice) Willie, you've got to get the
               carrot back to Topside. I know I sound strange.
               You would if there was a woman squeezing your
               onions and a dancing ferret outside.

Onion-Head ends the phone call.

Onion-Head: (still in a high-pitched voice) He's sending it with
               Formula One Taxis.
Vinnie: Daren't he come himself?
Onion-Head: (still in a high-pitched voice) No, in case you locked
               him in the Love-shed with me.

Lisa: Well he'd have nothing to worry about. You're all
               onion and no carrot.

The 17-FOOT PRIZE CARROT is thrown onto the allotment.

Vinnie: The carrot's arrived.
Lisa: Does that mean my time's up in the Love-shed?
Vinnie: You don't want to be around when his wife appears.
Onion-Head: What do you mean when my wife appears?
Vinnie: Oh, Albert always brings her down here after he's
               taken her out for lunch.
Onion-Head: That's not cricket. Because I nap his carrot, he naps
               my wife.
Lisa: But we got our carrot back.
Onion-Head: I'm not sure I want her back now I know she's been
               with Albert Jackson.
Lisa: You're a typical womaniser. It's ok for you to play the
               allotment, but you don't like your wife nibbling a bit
               of forbidden fruit.
Onion-Head: I wouldn't describe Albert Jackson as a fruit. More
               like last year's cabbage that's still not been dug up.
Lisa: But you ask any woman. It's not about cabbages, it's
               about carrots; and he's got a 17-footer.
Onion-Head: I'm telling you it's not real. He's been buying
               extension pieces from the fishing shop and covering
               them over with carrot-soup-painted papier-mâché.
Vinnie: If it's not real, how come you wanted to nap it?
Onion-Head: I wanted to stop a cheat.
Lisa: Now that really is a cucumber calling a lettuce green.
Onion-Head: How can I be green, when I'm an onion?
Vinnie: Of course you can have green onions – Booker T and
               the MGs did.
Onion-Head: Do you remember that song? That was 1962. Old hat
               these days at the garden club disco. All soil-heads
               want to rock the night away to now is some Red Hot
               Chilli Peppers.

Vinnie:	Whilst we're on the subject of discos, I want to ask you a question.
Onion-Head:	There's not one last dance I don't know, and not a woman safe if it's Kiss You All Over.
Lisa:	In your dreams. You've turned the Love-shed into a frigid den for eternal virgins.
Vinnie:	Can I ask my question before Albert gets here?
Onion-Head:	If he turns up with my wife, she'll have a go at me for being in the Love-shed, and I'll have a go at him for being with her.
Vinnie:	And I'll have a go at you if you don't answer this question.
Lisa:	I love a good fight.
Onion-Head:	I don't.
Vinnie:	Well, answer this question. Why did you always turn up at singles nights wearing your wedding ring?
Onion-Head:	Because I can't get it off.

Lisa takes hold of Onion-Head's left hand.

Lisa:	Here, let me try.
Onion-Head:	You won't get it off; it's super-super-glued on.
Vinnie:	What?
Onion-Head:	Punishment from the wife after the first time I ever strayed.
Lisa:	Did your wife buy it for you?
Onion-Head:	She did. She had a big win at the bingo just before we got married.
Lisa:	It must be thirty carat with a diamond in.
Vinnie:	Now that would be a carrot nap.
Lisa:	No Vinnie, it's spelt different.
Vinnie:	Not if you sell it to a chav.
Onion-Head:	You're not napping my ring.
Lisa:	I reckon we'd get it off with a strimmer.
Onion-Head:	You'd damage it.

Vinnie looks over to the water butt at the side of the Love-shed.

Vinnie:	What about if we emptied this water butt and put some penetrating oil in?
Lisa:	We'd need a lot to fill it.
Onion-Head:	You're not putting my hand in a water butt – that ferret you've got might fancy a drink.
Lisa:	No; he'll only fancy the top of your legs.
Vinnie:	Put just a drop of penetrating oil in at the bottom. Put Onion-Head in head first and leave the ring to soak for a couple of hours.
Onion-Head:	Please – I don't want to go in that butt. I'll get a headache if you put me in upside down.
Lisa:	Think of the double favour we'll be doing you.
Onion-Head:	Double, what do mean, double?
Vinnie:	Your wife won't see your face when she walks past.
Onion-Head:	She'll know my legs; she's slapped them enough.
Vinnie:	And minus the ring you can turn up at a singles night looking single.
Onion-Head:	No, some women prefer it if you're married. It's the flirtation with the forbidden that's the attraction.
Vinnie:	Well you never scored when I was on the door.
Onion-Head:	Too well known with the local Podpieces. They only wanted to know me when I had access to the Love-shed.
Lisa:	You'd be no good in it now on today's performance.
Onion-Head:	Don't you believe it. I'm having success these days in Bushby.
Lisa:	That's a bit upmarket. You'd need caviar, not carrots, to pull there.
Onion-Head:	And I've got a new pulling palace.
Vinnie:	Palace? They've not got a palace in Bushby – it's a castle.
Onion-Head:	More Buckingham than Windsor, the part I've took over.
Vinnie:	You're squatting in part of Bushby Castle?

Onion-Head: I don't declare it as my second home, but I've turned one of the dungeons into a love nest.

Lisa: Nobody goes down them dungeons. They're supposed to be haunted.

Vinnie: All over the local papers. More disappearances down the castle dungeons than the Bermuda Triangle.

Lisa: Only nobody knows anybody who's disappeared down there.

Vinnie: Somebody's doing one of them …

Lisa: Manipulating the media jobs.

Onion-Head: What are you looking at me for?

Vinnie: Because you're starting to look like a beetroot.

Lisa: If you've scared everyone in Bushby away, how do you get any Podpieces back to your Love Dungeon'?

Onion-Head: They're not Podpieces in Bushby.

Vinnie: You're right there. I once took a woman from Bushby out. She had three A-levels.

Onion-Head: Were they in before, during and after?

Vinnie: No shopping, spending and headaches.

Lisa: Good job I'm from Dipwick then.

Onion-Head: You'd like the dungeon.

Lisa: So what makes it better than the Love-shed?

Onion-Head: It's got a waterbed.

Vinnie: Bet that's why Albert's late. He's with Mrs Onion-Head making waves on it.

Onion-Head: I know Albert's never been there.

Vinnie: How do you know that?

Onion-Head: He would have seen where we hid the napped carrot.

Lisa: I bet some women got frightened when they saw the size of that.

Onion-Head: Not as frightened as when the rats started biting the waterbed.

Lisa: You weren't at the point of no return?

Onion-Head: No – I was too busy covering the carrot in rat poison.

Lisa and Vinnie look over to the prize carrot.

Lisa: That's covered in rat poison?
Vinnie: We could have eaten that.
Onion-Head: I didn't know you was going to nap it back.
Vinnie: Right; that ring's coming off or else you'll be eating
             carrot cake.
Onion-Head: Ok, Ok, pass me the penetrating oil.

Vinnie looks at his phone. Text Message Sound.

Vinnie: It's ok. No rush. Albert's just texted to say they
             won't be coming.
Lisa: Let me guess; Mrs Onion-Head's got a headache?
Vinnie: No, they've gone to sell a second-hand waterbed.
Onion-Head: They can't – I left my credit card in it.
Lisa: Vinnie, if Albert's not coming, why's he walking
             down here on his own?

Albert enters the allotment, waving his arms.

Albert: To nap that orange orgasm back, I've had to let
             Weed-killer Willie run off with Mrs Onion-Head.

Vinnie: But we don't want it back now; it's covered in
             rat poison.

Lisa: Vinnie, you speak for yourself. I think Albert could
             show me a better prize carrot in The Love-shed.

Lisa drags Albert into the Love-shed and locks the door.
Onion-Head begins to run off with Vinnie chasing him.

Vinnie: C'mon here, Onion-Head, I'm going to plant you!

END

(Green Onions music again)

Review of the Carrot Nappers from the Belper Short Play Festival Review

The Carrot Nappers is the latest play from the pen of the versatile and innovative Keith Large and concerns the theft of a seventeen-foot prize-winning carrot from an allotment set against the background of the aptly named Love Shed. It is both humorous and captivating, interlaced with mildly sexual connotations which only serve to enhance the flavour of the storyline. Albert Jackson, played by Jeff Stewart of "The Bill" fame, is the mild, affable, totally unruffled allotment worker, almost avuncular in character, who extolls the virtues of home-made cider amongst other things.

Vinnie Hollis, (Stuart Horobin) an unemployed bouncer and clearly agitated guardian of the giant carrot, is more than desirous to recover it, to say the least. Needless to say, he originally suspects Albert. The verbal altercations between these two protagonists set the tone for what clearly follows, when Vinnie chooses to enlist the help of former girlfriend Lisa (Carrie Hill) who promptly steals the show.

She is chosen as the matchmaker for Vinnie who, with her help, hopes to discover the culprit behind the theft. Lisa is subtly beguiling, full of feminine trickery interspersed with sexual charm, altogether the ideal personification of late 1960s glamour chic. The fact that this play is not set in that decade hardly matters.

With the allure of the allotment's "Love Shed" she sets the trap for Onion Head (Sean Glenn) whom Vinnie suspects is behind the theft of the giant carrot. Onion Head, despite his wildly exaggerated romantic notions, is a likeable character. He meets up with Lisa at the appointed rendezvous and subsequently, as one would expect, succumbs to her seductive charms before suspecting that someone is hiding in wait behind the shed.

After the ensuing scene in which Onion Head loses his trousers following a fight to retain his twelve-carat gold ring, Albert nonchalantly makes his reappearance. But is Albert the dark horse? Has he a secret to hide? And what is the significance of the much maligned water-bed?

Verdict: A well-crafted play with precise diction and diverse characterisation.

P. Watson
Belper Short Play Festival Official Reviewer

Conquer Stroke New Writing Night
Y Theatre, Leicester

TRYING a new cocktail is always an interesting experience.

The individual ingredients are fine, but what will they taste like when you put them all together?

That was my feeling attending Keith Large's Conquer Stroke New Writing Night at Leicester's Y Theatre.

Short plays mixed with monologues, local performers juggling for position with a couple of TV stars, I didn't know quite how it would all go down.

The result was challenging, dark and thought provoking moments complemented by a serious dash of laugh-out-loud - all in the best possible taste as a full house raised much-needed funds for the Stroke Association as they tackle the UK's fourth highest killer.

Delightful compere Lucy Kite, from Central TV introduced top of 'The Bill' Jeff Stewart who was more Tommy Cooper than Reg Hollis in his one-man act – a nutcase with a suitcase, he turned the potentially naff into a great laugh. Little short of brilliant.

The 'local' fare was excellent too. Loughborough woman Clare Devine directed several of Keith Large's pieces including the horrors of The Garage with Leah Georges outstanding in the lead role and We didn't know you were Coming, a showcase for the talents of Amy Allen.

Particularly memorable was Brian Fury's immensely powerful monologue highlighting life's outrageous misfortune.

Shelley Draper lightened the mood in Zumba and the evening was rounded off on a high by Miriam, a missionary with human failings brought to life by Lesley Emery.

A truly memorable cocktail – looking forward already to the next of Keith's creations.

John Brindley - March 2016

Footnote: Zumba was written by Sheila Kondras
Miriam was written by Steven Lancefield
Special thanks to the talent of Leicester based Phoenix Writers and the Shardlow charm of Gabriel Lockwood and Peter McManus for making such a wonderful night possible.

STROKE ASSOCIATION

Stroke Association is the leading charity in the UK changing the world for people affected by stroke.

In the last 20 years the number of people dying of stroke has halved while the number of major strokes has decreased by 40 per cent. More people than ever are benefitting from cutting-edge treatments and making full recoveries. And more people now understand the need to seek emergency treatment for stroke.

We've been at the heart of every one of these developments, championing the cause of stroke and stroke survivors.

Our research has helped to improve treatments and care which has saved tens of thousands of lives.

Our support services have helped hundreds of thousands of people get through one of the most frightening experiences of their lives and build a life after stroke.

And our campaigning has touched the lives of even more people through initiatives like the FAST campaign which we developed to help people recognise the signs of a stroke and take emergency action. The Department of Health in England was so impressed with this campaign that they took it up in 2009 and promoted to millions of people.

But there's still more to do. Every year there are about 152,000 strokes in the UK. Thanks to improvements to stroke care you are twice as likely to survive a stroke than 20 years ago, however stroke remains the fourth single largest cause of death in the UK.

As the leading stroke charity in the UK we know we need to change how people think about this devastating disease. But we can't do it on our own. We need to work with people who share our commitment to changing the world for people affected by stroke - with stroke survivors and their families; with decision makers; with researchers and medics; as well as with our supporters - so that we can ensure stroke gets the attention it deserves.

At the Stroke Association we believe that strokes can and should be prevented.

- We believe that everyone has the right to make the best recovery they can from stroke.

- We believe in the power of research to save lives and ensure people make the best recovery they can.
- And ultimately, we believe that together we can change the world for people affected by stroke.
- We are for life after stroke.

If you have been affected by stroke, if you share our passion to change the world for people affected by stroke, if you share our beliefs, then please do join with us.

Together we can conquer stroke.

www.stroke.org.uk